The Little Story of the Number

4

BY ELIZABETH POLLOCK

This special story was written from my wonderful experiences in working and raising children. It is dedicated to my children, Jeff and Nastacha, who have inspired me to write this story.

I want to thank Elsa Jackson from Corpus Christi who reviewed this book, David Montana from Bogota for the beautiful art work and my family for their unconditional support.

My sincere wish is that you and your children enjoy reading this story as much as I have enjoyed putting it together.

Elizabeth Pollock

Nastacha, a little girl four years old lived in Lima, Peru. She was so interested in the number 4 that she was always thinking about it. She thought about its shape and the sound of saying the number 4. One night on the 4th month of the year 2013 she went to bed. In the middle of a clear, quiet night with the moon shining, she heard the echo of 4 owls. The owls lived in the tree close to her window. The sound was so clear and pretty that she went into sleep and started to dream.

In her dream, Nastacha was in the far Lands of the Peruvian Andes, in the pampa where 4 llamas lived. The territory was emerald green with grass, so the 4 llamas stopped to eat all the time. On top of the mountain chain, she could see the 4 noisy llamas with their tall necks, long legs and full of beautiful fur. They were calling the number that she was always thinking about, "4! 4! 4!". Oh, she loved the sound of counting to 4 over and over again.

Suddenly, a storm was developing outside her room. The sound of the rain woke her up, but she went right back to sleep, and began dreaming again. She found herself counting again, 1, 2, 3, 4; 1,2,3,4. This time the scenery had changed. She saw 4 soccer balls. Nastacha knew that she had always wanted to be a soccer player. She had 4 soccer little friends. She saw images of the number 4 and kept listening to the sound of the soccer balls and started kicking them. The rain outside of her window got stronger. She felt like she was tied to her bed, but instead, she was tangled in her blankets. Reaching for the blankets she woke up. The alarm clock was ringing, and it was time to go to school.

She went to class and got to play soccer with her 4 friends. She went to school to be a good student, but it was more fun to play with her 4 little friends and 4 soccer balls. She wanted to learn to be the best girl soccer player. The day went by and she came back from school. She went to bed and again fell into a deep sleep.

This time, the dream took her to Bogota, the capital of Colombia, in South America. The school was located 4 miles from the chain of mountains. There were lakes and little bodies of beautiful crystal water. The weather was chilly and she loved it. About 4 miles away from the school, she saw a chapel and tried to walk to it. She met the 4 nuns that once taught her how to count to 4 and pray every morning. She asked them if they could take her to a place where she could be the best soccer player in school. The nuns talked to each other and the one named Lisa said, "Of course you can be the best soccer player in school. However, first you have to promise that you will count to four and much higher, and you will learn to write all the numbers. This way you can not only be the best soccer player, but a very good student as well." Then she woke up as she heard her Mother calling her for supper.

Christmas was fast approaching and Nastacha decided that after dreaming about all these things, she really wanted to ask Santa for something very special. There was something very special about the number 4 because it was always included in her dream adventures. The following night, she did not want to go to sleep and dream of far lands in South America, mountains and lakes, and the mystery of the number 4. She wrote a letter to Santa that she wanted to go to Brazil in South America to watch the 2014 soccer world cup event. She wanted to see in reality many number 4s on the jerseys of many fabulous soccer players.

On the 24th of December that year, Dad gave her an envelope that contained 4 tickets. He said, "My little dreamer, this is for you. Santa delivered this letter and this yellow manila envelope with a map of Brazil." The envelope contained reservations for her and her brother Jeff, and her Mom & Dad, to go to the 2014 Soccer World Cup event. She was very, very happy. Her dream had finally come true.